THE BARIATRIC SMOOTHIE COOKBOOK

CLARA WILSON

COPYRIGHT©

All rights reserved. No part of this book may be reproduced, stored in a retrieval system, or transmitted in any form or by any means, electronic, mechanical, photocopying, recording, or otherwise, without the prior written permission of the author.

Table of Contents

UNDERSTANDING BARIATRIC SURGERY AND NUTRITION 7

The Rise of Bariatric Surgery 7

Types of Bariatric Surgery 8

Nutritional Considerations Before and After Bariatric Surgery 10

Challenges and Adaptations in Bariatric Nutrition 13

BENEFITS OF INCORPORATING SMOOTHIES INTO YOUR DIET 16

TIPS FOR CREATING BARIATRIC-FRIENDLY SMOOTHIES 25

RECIPES 34

1. Green Protein Power Smoothie 34

2. Berry Blast Smoothie 36

3. Creamy Peanut Butter Banana Smoothie.. 38

4. Chocolate Avocado Protein Shake ... 40

5. Tropical Mango Coconut Smoothie .. 42

6. Vanilla Almond Protein Smoothie 44

7. Kale Pineapple Green Smoothie 46

8. Blueberry Almond Spinach Smoothie 48

9. Peach Mango Protein Shake 50

10. Raspberry Coconut Chia Smoothie. 52

11. Spinach Apple Ginger Smoothie 54

12. Banana Nut Protein Shake 56

13. Kiwi Lime Green Smoothie 58

14. Chocolate Cherry Almond Smoothie 60

15. Pineapple Coconut Protein Shake .. 62

16. Mango Turmeric Smoothie 64

17. Raspberry Lemonade Smoothie..... 66

18. Vanilla Berry Chia Smoothie 68

19. Green Apple Kale Smoothie.......... 70

20. Peanut Butter Chocolate Banana Smoothie....................................... 72

21. Coconut Berry Protein Shake........ 74

22. Pumpkin Spice Protein Smoothie... 76

23. Mint Chocolate Chip Smoothie 78

24. Strawberry Banana Oat Smoothie . 80

UNDERSTANDING BARIATRIC SURGERY AND NUTRITION

Bariatric surgery, often regarded as a transformative tool in the fight against obesity, is a procedure that alters the digestive system to help individuals achieve significant weight loss. While the surgery itself is a crucial step, understanding the intricacies of bariatric surgery and its impact on nutrition is essential for long-term success and optimal health outcomes. In this exploration, we delve into the various aspects of bariatric surgery, its different types, and the profound implications it has on nutritional intake and dietary habits.

The Rise of Bariatric Surgery

The prevalence of obesity has surged in recent decades, posing significant health risks and challenges worldwide. Bariatric surgery emerged as a viable solution for individuals with severe obesity who struggled to achieve sustainable weight loss through conventional methods such as diet and exercise. Initially considered a drastic measure, bariatric surgery has evolved into a safe and effective intervention, offering hope to those grappling with obesity-related health issues.

Types of Bariatric Surgery

Bariatric surgery encompasses several procedures, each designed to achieve weight loss through different mechanisms. The most common types include:

- Gastric Bypass: This procedure involves creating a smaller stomach pouch and rerouting the digestive tract to bypass a portion of the small intestine. By reducing stomach capacity and altering nutrient absorption, gastric bypass promotes weight loss and metabolic changes.

- Sleeve Gastrectomy: During a sleeve gastrectomy, a large portion of the stomach is surgically removed, leaving a smaller, banana-shaped sleeve. This restricts food intake and reduces hunger hormones, facilitating weight loss.

- Gastric Banding: Also known as laparoscopic adjustable gastric banding, this procedure involves placing an inflatable band around the upper part of the stomach to create a small pouch. By restricting food intake and promoting satiety, gastric banding aids in weight loss.

- Biliopancreatic Diversion with Duodenal Switch (BPD/DS): BPD/DS combines aspects of gastric bypass and sleeve gastrectomy. It involves removing a portion of the stomach and rerouting the intestines to limit food absorption, resulting in substantial weight loss.

Nutritional Considerations Before and After Bariatric Surgery

Before undergoing bariatric surgery, patients typically undergo thorough evaluations and counseling to understand the dietary and lifestyle changes required for success. Pre-surgery nutrition interventions aim to optimize health, facilitate weight loss, and prepare individuals for the post-operative phase. This often involves adopting a low-calorie, high-protein diet to reduce liver size and enhance surgical outcomes.

Following surgery, patients undergo a gradual transition from liquid to solid foods, guided by healthcare professionals and registered dietitians. The post-operative diet is meticulously designed to ensure adequate nutrient intake while supporting healing and weight loss. Key nutritional considerations after bariatric surgery include:

- Protein Intake: Protein plays a crucial role in preserving lean body mass, promoting wound healing, and supporting metabolic function. Bariatric patients are advised to prioritize protein-rich foods such as lean meats, poultry, fish, eggs, dairy, and plant-based sources.

- Hydration: Adequate hydration is essential for optimal recovery and overall health. Bariatric surgery can alter fluid absorption, making it imperative for patients to consume sufficient fluids throughout the day. Water, herbal teas, and sugar-free beverages are encouraged, while carbonated and sugary drinks should be avoided.

- Vitamin and Mineral Supplementation: Bariatric surgery can compromise nutrient absorption, leading to deficiencies in vitamins and minerals such as vitamin B12, iron, calcium, and vitamin D. Patients are prescribed specialized multivitamin and mineral supplements to prevent deficiencies and promote long-term health.

- Portion Control and Meal Frequency: Bariatric patients must adhere to portion control guidelines and eat smaller, more frequent meals to accommodate their reduced stomach capacity. This helps prevent discomfort, promotes satiety, and facilitates weight loss maintenance.

Challenges and Adaptations in Bariatric Nutrition

While bariatric surgery offers numerous benefits, adapting to the dietary changes post-surgery can pose challenges for patients. Common issues include difficulty tolerating certain foods, gastrointestinal discomfort, and emotional eating habits. To overcome these obstacles and achieve sustainable success, individuals must develop mindful eating practices, cultivate a supportive environment, and seek ongoing guidance from healthcare professionals.

In addition to dietary modifications, adopting a holistic approach to health and wellness is essential for long-term bariatric success. This includes regular physical activity, stress management techniques, behavioral counseling, and peer support groups. By addressing the physical, emotional, and social aspects of weight loss, individuals can enhance their overall well-being and maintain their progress over time.

Bariatric surgery represents a significant milestone in the treatment of obesity, offering hope and transformation to individuals struggling with excess weight and related health issues. However, successful outcomes rely heavily on understanding the complex interplay between bariatric surgery and nutrition. By embracing dietary modifications, prioritizing nutrient-rich foods, and adopting a holistic approach to health, bariatric patients can embark on a journey towards improved well-being and lasting weight loss success. Through education, support, and personalized guidance, individuals can navigate the challenges of bariatric nutrition with confidence and resilience, ultimately achieving their health and wellness goals.

BENEFITS OF INCORPORATING SMOOTHIES INTO YOUR DIET

Smoothies have emerged as popular dietary staples for health-conscious individuals seeking convenient and nutritious meal options. These blended beverages offer a myriad of benefits, ranging from enhanced nutrient intake to improved digestion and hydration. In this comprehensive exploration, we delve into the numerous advantages of incorporating smoothies into your diet and how they can contribute to overall health and well-being.

1. Nutrient-Rich Ingredients

One of the primary benefits of smoothies is their ability to pack a diverse array of nutrients into a single serving. By combining fruits, vegetables, leafy greens, nuts, seeds, and other wholesome ingredients, smoothies offer a concentrated source of vitamins, minerals, antioxidants, and phytonutrients essential for optimal health. Consuming a nutrient-rich diet is associated with numerous health benefits, including reduced risk of chronic diseases such as heart disease, diabetes, and certain cancers.

2. Increased Fruit and Vegetable Consumption

Many individuals struggle to meet the recommended daily intake of fruits and vegetables. Smoothies provide a convenient and delicious way to boost fruit and vegetable consumption, making it easier to achieve the recommended servings per day. Whether blended into a refreshing fruit smoothie or incorporated into a green smoothie packed with leafy greens, fruits, and vegetables, smoothies offer a simple solution for increasing dietary diversity and promoting overall health.

3. Improved Digestion and Gut Health

Smoothies can support digestive health by providing a concentrated source of dietary fiber, which promotes regularity and bowel function. Fiber-rich ingredients such as fruits, vegetables, and seeds aid in digestion, prevent constipation, and support the growth of beneficial gut bacteria. Additionally, smoothies containing probiotic-rich ingredients such as yogurt or kefir can further enhance gut health by introducing beneficial bacteria into the digestive tract, supporting immune function and nutrient absorption.

4. Hydration and Fluid Balance

Maintaining adequate hydration is essential for overall health and well-being. Smoothies, particularly those made with water, coconut water, or unsweetened almond milk, contribute to daily fluid intake and support hydration. Hydrating smoothies are especially beneficial during hot weather or after physical activity when fluid needs are heightened. Adding hydrating ingredients such as cucumber, watermelon, or citrus fruits can further enhance the hydrating properties of smoothies, keeping you feeling refreshed and revitalized.

5. Weight Management and Satiety

Smoothies can be an effective tool for weight management when incorporated into a balanced diet. Blending whole fruits, vegetables, and protein-rich ingredients such as Greek yogurt, tofu, or protein powder into a smoothie can create a satisfying meal replacement that helps control hunger and prevent overeating. Consuming a nutrient-dense smoothie as part of a meal or snack can promote feelings of fullness and satiety, reducing the likelihood of unhealthy snacking and supporting weight loss or weight maintenance goals.

6. Quick and Convenient Meal Option

In today's fast-paced world, convenience is paramount when it comes to meal preparation. Smoothies offer a quick and easy meal option that can be prepared in minutes and enjoyed on the go. Whether you're rushing out the door in the morning or need a nutritious snack between meetings, smoothies provide a portable and customizable solution for busy lifestyles. With minimal prep time and no cooking required, smoothies are ideal for individuals seeking nutritious meals without the hassle of traditional cooking.

7. Versatility and Customization

One of the most appealing aspects of smoothies is their versatility and adaptability to individual tastes and dietary preferences. With countless ingredient combinations and flavor profiles to choose from, smoothies can be customized to suit a wide range of dietary needs and flavor preferences. Whether you prefer sweet and fruity, creamy and indulgent, or green and refreshing, there's a smoothie recipe to satisfy every palate. Additionally, smoothies can easily accommodate dietary restrictions such as dairy-free, gluten-free, or vegan, making them inclusive options for diverse populations.

8. Boosted Energy and Vitality

Consuming a nutrient-dense smoothie can provide a natural energy boost and enhance overall vitality. The combination of vitamins, minerals, antioxidants, and phytonutrients found in smoothie ingredients supports cellular energy production, cognitive function, and physical performance. Smoothies made with energy-boosting ingredients such as leafy greens, berries, nuts, and seeds can help combat fatigue, improve mental clarity, and enhance overall well-being, making them an ideal choice for starting your day on a positive note.

9. Enhanced Immune Function

A well-nourished body is better equipped to fend off illness and infections. Smoothies rich in immune-boosting nutrients such as vitamin C, vitamin E, zinc, and antioxidants can strengthen the immune system and promote resilience against pathogens. Ingredients such as citrus fruits, berries, kiwi, spinach, ginger, and turmeric are known for their immune-supportive properties and can be incorporated into delicious smoothie recipes to help keep you healthy and vibrant year-round.

10. Support for Healthy Aging

As we age, maintaining optimal nutrition becomes increasingly important for preserving health and vitality. Smoothies can play a valuable role in supporting healthy aging by providing essential nutrients that support brain function, bone health, cardiovascular health, and overall longevity. Incorporating nutrient-rich ingredients such as leafy greens, berries, nuts, seeds, and omega-3 fatty acids into smoothies can help protect against age-related decline and promote lifelong wellness.

Incorporating smoothies into your diet offers a multitude of benefits for overall health and well-being. From providing essential nutrients and supporting digestion to promoting hydration, weight management, and energy levels, smoothies are a convenient and delicious way to nourish your body and enhance your quality of life. By experimenting with different ingredients and flavors, customizing recipes to suit your preferences, and enjoying smoothies as part of a balanced diet, you can harness the power of these nutrient-packed beverages to optimize your health and vitality for years to come.

TIPS FOR CREATING BARIATRIC-FRIENDLY SMOOTHIES

Bariatric surgery represents a significant step in the journey toward weight loss and improved health for individuals struggling with obesity. Following bariatric surgery, dietary adjustments are necessary to support healing, promote weight loss, and prevent complications. Smoothies offer a convenient and nutritious option for bariatric patients, providing a concentrated source of essential nutrients in a palatable and easily digestible form. In this guide, we'll explore tips for creating bariatric-friendly smoothies that are well-suited to the unique needs and dietary restrictions of individuals post-bariatric surgery.

1. Prioritize Protein

Protein is a critical nutrient for bariatric patients, as it supports wound healing, preserves lean muscle mass, and promotes satiety. When creating bariatric-friendly smoothies, prioritize protein-rich ingredients to ensure adequate intake. Opt for high-quality protein sources such as Greek yogurt, cottage cheese, silken tofu, protein powder (whey, casein, or plant-based), and skim milk. Aim to include at least 15-20 grams of protein per smoothie serving to support optimal nutrition and weight management goals.

2. Choose Low-Sugar Fruits

While fruits are nutritious and packed with vitamins and minerals, some varieties can be high in natural sugars, which may not be well-tolerated post-bariatric surgery. Choose lower-sugar fruits such as berries (strawberries, blueberries, raspberries), kiwi, citrus fruits (orange, grapefruit), and melons (watermelon, cantaloupe) for your smoothies. These fruits provide sweetness and flavor without causing rapid spikes in blood sugar levels, making them suitable choices for bariatric patients.

3. Incorporate Vegetables

Vegetables are an excellent addition to bariatric-friendly smoothies, providing fiber, vitamins, minerals, and antioxidants without excess calories or carbohydrates. Leafy greens such as spinach, kale, and Swiss chard are particularly nutrient-dense and can be blended seamlessly into smoothies without altering the taste. Other vegetable options include cucumber, celery, carrots, and zucchini. Experiment with different combinations to find the perfect balance of flavors and nutrients in your smoothies.

4. Include Healthy Fats

Healthy fats are essential for bariatric patients as they support nutrient absorption, hormone production, and overall health. Incorporating sources of healthy fats into your smoothies can enhance satiety and promote a feeling of fullness. Additions such as avocado, nut butter (almond, peanut, cashew), chia seeds, flaxseeds, and coconut oil are excellent options for boosting the nutritional profile of your smoothies. Be mindful of portion sizes, as fats are calorie-dense and can contribute to excess calorie intake if consumed in large quantities.

5. Limit Added Sugars and Sweeteners

Added sugars and sweeteners should be used sparingly in bariatric-friendly smoothies to avoid unnecessary calories and potential digestive discomfort. Instead of sweetening your smoothies with sugar, honey, or syrups, opt for natural sweeteners such as stevia, monk fruit, or erythritol, which provide sweetness without the added calories or carbohydrates. Alternatively, rely on the natural sweetness of fruits and vegetables to flavor your smoothies without the need for additional sweeteners.

6. Experiment with Texture and Consistency

Texture and consistency play a crucial role in the palatability of bariatric-friendly smoothies. For individuals with sensitive stomachs or newly operated digestive systems, it's essential to blend smoothies to a smooth and creamy consistency to prevent discomfort and ensure easy digestion. Experiment with different blending techniques, such as adding ice cubes or frozen fruits for a thicker texture or incorporating liquids such as water, almond milk, or coconut water to adjust the consistency to your preference.

7. Pay Attention to Portion Sizes

Portion control is key when incorporating smoothies into a bariatric diet. While smoothies can be a convenient and nutritious meal option, it's important to consume them in moderation and avoid overeating. Stick to single-serving portions and be mindful of calorie and nutrient content when preparing your smoothies. Use measuring cups or a kitchen scale to portion out ingredients accurately and avoid excess calories or carbohydrates that may impede weight loss progress.

8. Consider Nutrient Supplementation

Bariatric surgery can impact nutrient absorption, leading to deficiencies in vitamins and minerals such as vitamin B12, iron, calcium, and vitamin D. To ensure optimal nutrition and prevent deficiencies, consider incorporating specialized bariatric-friendly vitamin and mineral supplements into your smoothies. Choose supplements specifically formulated for bariatric patients, and follow your healthcare provider's recommendations regarding timing and dosage.

9. Listen to Your Body

Lastly, listen to your body and pay attention to how different ingredients and combinations affect your digestion, energy levels, and overall well-being. Every individual's dietary needs and tolerance levels may vary, so it's essential to tailor your smoothie recipes to suit your specific preferences and requirements. If certain ingredients or textures cause discomfort or digestive issues, adjust your smoothie recipes accordingly and prioritize ingredients that promote optimal digestion and nutrient absorption.

Creating bariatric-friendly smoothies can be a delicious and convenient way to support your nutritional needs and weight loss goals post-bariatric surgery. By prioritizing protein, choosing nutrient-dense ingredients, limiting added sugars, and paying attention to portion sizes and texture, you can enjoy flavorful and satisfying smoothies that promote healing, support weight management, and enhance overall health and well-being. Experiment with different recipes and ingredient combinations to find the perfect balance of taste, nutrition, and digestibility for your individual needs.

RECIPES

1. Green Protein Power Smoothie

Ingredients:

- 1 cup spinach
- 1/2 ripe avocado
- 1/2 cup Greek yogurt
- 1/4 cup unsweetened almond milk
- 1 scoop vanilla protein powder
- 1 tablespoon chia seeds
- 1/2 teaspoon cinnamon
- Ice cubes (optional)

Instructions:

- In a blender, combine spinach, avocado, Greek yogurt, almond milk, protein powder, chia seeds, and cinnamon.

- Blend until smooth and creamy.

- Add ice cubes if desired and blend again until well incorporated.

- Pour into a glass and enjoy immediately.

2. Berry Blast Smoothie

Ingredients:

- 1/2 cup mixed berries (strawberries, blueberries, raspberries)

- 1/2 ripe banana

- 1/2 cup unsweetened coconut water

- 1/4 cup silken tofu

- 1 tablespoon honey or agave nectar

- 1/4 teaspoon vanilla extract

- Ice cubes (optional)

Instructions:

- Place mixed berries, banana, coconut water, silken tofu, honey or agave nectar, and vanilla extract in a blender.

- Blend until smooth and creamy.

- Add ice cubes if desired and blend again until well combined.

- Pour into a glass and serve immediately.

3. Creamy Peanut Butter Banana Smoothie

Ingredients:

- 1 ripe banana
- 2 tablespoons creamy peanut butter
- 1/2 cup unsweetened almond milk
- 1/4 cup Greek yogurt
- 1 tablespoon flaxseed meal
- 1/2 teaspoon honey or maple syrup (optional)
- Ice cubes (optional)

Instructions:

- In a blender, combine banana, peanut butter, almond milk, Greek yogurt, flaxseed meal, and honey or maple syrup (if using).

- Blend until smooth and creamy.

- Add ice cubes if desired and blend again until well incorporated.

- Pour into a glass and enjoy immediately.

4. Chocolate Avocado Protein Shake

Ingredients:

- 1/2 ripe avocado
- 1 tablespoon unsweetened cocoa powder
- 1 scoop chocolate protein powder
- 1/2 cup unsweetened almond milk
- 1/4 cup Greek yogurt
- 1 tablespoon honey or agave nectar

- Ice cubes (optional)

Instructions:

- Place avocado, cocoa powder, protein powder, almond milk, Greek yogurt, and honey or agave nectar in a blender.
- Blend until smooth and creamy.
- Add ice cubes if desired and blend again until well combined.
- Pour into a glass and serve immediately.

5. Tropical Mango Coconut Smoothie

Ingredients:

- 1/2 cup frozen mango chunks
- 1/4 cup canned coconut milk (light)
- 1/2 ripe banana
- 1/4 cup Greek yogurt
- 1 tablespoon shredded coconut

- 1/4 teaspoon vanilla extract

- Ice cubes (optional)

Instructions:

- In a blender, combine frozen mango chunks, coconut milk, banana, Greek yogurt, shredded coconut, and vanilla extract.

- Blend until smooth and creamy.

- Add ice cubes if desired and blend again until well incorporated.

- Pour into a glass and enjoy immediately.

6. Vanilla Almond Protein Smoothie

Ingredients:

- 1/2 cup unsweetened almond milk
- 1/2 cup Greek yogurt
- 1 scoop vanilla protein powder
- 1 tablespoon almond butter

- 1/4 teaspoon vanilla extract

- Ice cubes (optional)

Instructions:

- Place almond milk, Greek yogurt, protein powder, almond butter, and vanilla extract in a blender.

- Blend until smooth and creamy.

- Add ice cubes if desired and blend again until well combined.

- Pour into a glass and serve immediately.

7. Kale Pineapple Green Smoothie

Ingredients:

- 1 cup chopped kale (stems removed)
- 1/2 cup frozen pineapple chunks
- 1/2 ripe banana

- 1/2 cup unsweetened coconut water

- 1 tablespoon lime juice

- 1 tablespoon honey or agave nectar

- Ice cubes (optional)

Instructions:

- In a blender, combine chopped kale, frozen pineapple chunks, banana, coconut water, lime juice, and honey or agave nectar.

- Blend until smooth and creamy.

- Add ice cubes if desired and blend again until well incorporated.

- Pour into a glass and enjoy immediately.

8. Blueberry Almond Spinach Smoothie

Ingredients:

- 1/2 cup fresh spinach

- 1/2 cup frozen blueberries

- 1/2 ripe banana

- 1/2 cup unsweetened almond milk

- 1 tablespoon almond butter

- 1 tablespoon flaxseed meal

- Ice cubes (optional)

Instructions:

- Place spinach, blueberries, banana, almond milk, almond butter, and flaxseed meal in a blender.

- Blend until smooth and creamy.

- Add ice cubes if desired and blend again until well combined.

- Pour into a glass and serve immediately.

9. Peach Mango Protein Shake

Ingredients:

- 1/2 cup frozen peach slices
- 1/2 cup frozen mango chunks

- 1/2 cup unsweetened almond milk

- 1/4 cup Greek yogurt

- 1 scoop vanilla protein powder

- 1 tablespoon honey or agave nectar

- Ice cubes (optional)

Instructions:

- In a blender, combine frozen peach slices, frozen mango chunks, almond milk, Greek yogurt, protein powder, and honey or agave nectar.

- Blend until smooth and creamy.

- Add ice cubes if desired and blend again until well incorporated.

- Pour into a glass and enjoy immediately.

10. Raspberry Coconut Chia Smoothie

Ingredients:

- 1/2 cup fresh raspberries

- 1/2 ripe banana

- 1/4 cup canned coconut milk (light)

- 1 tablespoon chia seeds

- 1/4 teaspoon vanilla extract

- Ice cubes (optional)

Instructions:

- In a blender, combine raspberries, banana, coconut milk, chia seeds, and vanilla extract.

- Blend until smooth and creamy.

- Add ice cubes if desired and blend again until well combined.

- Pour into a glass and serve immediately.

11. Spinach Apple Ginger Smoothie

Ingredients:

- 1 cup fresh spinach
- 1 medium apple, cored and chopped
- 1/2-inch piece of fresh ginger, peeled
- 1/2 cup unsweetened almond milk
- 1 tablespoon honey or agave nectar
- 1/4 teaspoon ground cinnamon
- Ice cubes (optional)

Instructions:

- Place spinach, chopped apple, fresh ginger, almond milk, honey or agave nectar, and ground cinnamon in a blender.
- Blend until smooth and creamy.

- Add ice cubes if desired and blend again until well combined.

- Pour into a glass and enjoy immediately.

12. Banana Nut Protein Shake

Ingredients:

- 1 ripe banana
- 1/4 cup unsweetened almond milk
- 1/4 cup Greek yogurt
- 1 scoop vanilla protein powder
- 1 tablespoon almond butter
- 1 tablespoon chopped walnuts
- Ice cubes (optional)

Instructions:

- In a blender, combine ripe banana, almond milk, Greek yogurt, protein powder, almond butter, and chopped walnuts.

- Blend until smooth and creamy.

- Add ice cubes if desired and blend again until well incorporated.

- Pour into a glass and serve immediately.

13. Kiwi Lime Green Smoothie

Ingredients:

- 2 kiwis, peeled and sliced
- Juice of 1 lime
- 1/2 cup fresh spinach
- 1/2 cup unsweetened coconut water
- 1 tablespoon honey or agave nectar
- Ice cubes (optional)

Instructions:

- Place sliced kiwis, lime juice, spinach, coconut water, and honey or agave nectar in a blender.
- Blend until smooth and creamy.

- Add ice cubes if desired and blend again until well combined.

- Pour into a glass and enjoy immediately.

14. Chocolate Cherry Almond Smoothie

Ingredients:

- 1/2 cup frozen cherries
- 1 tablespoon unsweetened cocoa powder
- 1/2 ripe banana
- 1/2 cup unsweetened almond milk
- 1/4 cup Greek yogurt
- 1 tablespoon almond butter
- Ice cubes (optional)

Instructions:

- In a blender, combine frozen cherries, cocoa powder, ripe banana, almond milk, Greek yogurt, and almond butter.

- Blend until smooth and creamy.

- Add ice cubes if desired and blend again until well incorporated.

- Pour into a glass and serve immediately.

15. Pineapple Coconut Protein Shake

Ingredients:

- 1/2 cup frozen pineapple chunks
- 1/4 cup canned coconut milk (light)
- 1/2 cup unsweetened almond milk
- 1 scoop vanilla protein powder
- 1 tablespoon shredded coconut
- Ice cubes (optional)

Instructions:

- In a blender, combine frozen pineapple chunks, coconut milk, almond milk, protein powder, and shredded coconut.

- Blend until smooth and creamy.

- Add ice cubes if desired and blend again until well combined.

- Pour into a glass and enjoy immediately.

16. Mango Turmeric Smoothie

Ingredients:

- 1/2 cup frozen mango chunks
- 1/2-inch piece of fresh turmeric, peeled
- 1/2 cup unsweetened coconut water
- 1/4 cup Greek yogurt
- 1 tablespoon honey or agave nectar

- Ice cubes (optional)

Instructions:

- Place frozen mango chunks, fresh turmeric, coconut water, Greek yogurt, and honey or agave nectar in a blender.

- Blend until smooth and creamy.

- Add ice cubes if desired and blend again until well combined.

- Pour into a glass and serve immediately.

17. Raspberry Lemonade Smoothie

Ingredients:

- 1/2 cup fresh raspberries

- Juice of 1 lemon

- 1/2 cup unsweetened almond milk

- 1/4 cup Greek yogurt

- 1 tablespoon honey or agave nectar

- Ice cubes (optional)

Instructions:

- In a blender, combine fresh raspberries, lemon juice, almond milk, Greek yogurt, and honey or agave nectar.

- Blend until smooth and creamy.

- Add ice cubes if desired and blend again until well combined.

- Pour into a glass and enjoy immediately.

18. Vanilla Berry Chia Smoothie

Ingredients:

- 1/2 cup mixed berries (strawberries, blueberries, raspberries)

- 1/2 cup unsweetened almond milk

- 1/4 cup Greek yogurt

- 1 tablespoon chia seeds

- 1/4 teaspoon vanilla extract

- Ice cubes (optional)

Instructions:

- Place mixed berries, almond milk, Greek yogurt, chia seeds, and vanilla extract in a blender.

- Blend until smooth and creamy.

- Add ice cubes if desired and blend again until well combined.

- Pour into a glass and serve immediately.

19. Green Apple Kale Smoothie

Ingredients:

- 1 medium green apple, cored and chopped
- 1 cup chopped kale (stems removed)
- 1/2 cup unsweetened coconut water
- 1/4 cup Greek yogurt
- 1 tablespoon honey or agave nectar
- Ice cubes (optional)

Instructions:

- In a blender, combine chopped green apple, chopped kale, coconut water, Greek yogurt, and honey or agave nectar.

- Blend until smooth and creamy.

- Add ice cubes if desired and blend again until well combined.

- Pour into a glass and enjoy immediately.

20. Peanut Butter Chocolate Banana Smoothie

Ingredients:

- 1 ripe banana

- 2 tablespoons creamy peanut butter

- 1 tablespoon unsweetened cocoa powder

- 1/2 cup unsweetened almond milk

- 1/4 cup Greek yogurt

- Ice cubes (optional)

Instructions:

- In a blender, combine ripe banana, peanut butter, cocoa powder, almond milk, and Greek yogurt.

- Blend until smooth and creamy.

- Add ice cubes if desired and blend again until well combined.

- Pour into a glass and serve immediately.

21. Coconut Berry Protein Shake

Ingredients:

- 1/2 cup mixed berries (strawberries, blueberries, raspberries)

- 1/4 cup canned coconut milk (light)

- 1/2 cup unsweetened almond milk

- 1 scoop vanilla protein powder

- 1 tablespoon shredded coconut

- Ice cubes (optional)

Instructions:

- In a blender, combine mixed berries, coconut milk, almond milk, protein powder, and shredded coconut.

- Blend until smooth and creamy.

- Add ice cubes if desired and blend again until well combined.

- Pour into a glass and enjoy immediately.

22. Pumpkin Spice Protein Smoothie

Ingredients:

- 1/4 cup canned pumpkin puree
- 1/2 ripe banana
- 1/2 cup unsweetened almond milk
- 1 scoop vanilla protein powder
- 1/4 teaspoon pumpkin pie spice

- 1 tablespoon honey or agave nectar
- Ice cubes (optional)

Instructions:

- In a blender, combine pumpkin puree, ripe banana, almond milk, protein powder, pumpkin pie spice, and honey or agave nectar.
- Blend until smooth and creamy.
- Add ice cubes if desired and blend again until well combined.
- Pour into a glass and serve immediately.

23. Mint Chocolate Chip Smoothie

Ingredients:

- 1/2 ripe avocado
- 1 tablespoon unsweetened cocoa powder
- 1/4 teaspoon peppermint extract
- 1/2 cup unsweetened almond milk

- 1/4 cup Greek yogurt

- 1 tablespoon honey or agave nectar

- Ice cubes (optional)

Instructions:

- In a blender, combine ripe avocado, cocoa powder, peppermint extract, almond milk, Greek yogurt, and honey or agave nectar.

- Blend until smooth and creamy.

- Add ice cubes if desired and blend again until well combined.

- Pour into a glass and serve immediately.

24. Strawberry Banana Oat Smoothie

Ingredients:

- 1/2 cup frozen strawberries

- 1/2 ripe banana

- 1/4 cup rolled oats

- 1/2 cup unsweetened almond milk

- 1/4 cup Greek yogurt

- 1 tablespoon honey or agave nectar

- Ice cubes (optional)

Instructions:

- In a blender, combine frozen strawberries, ripe banana, rolled oats, almond milk, Greek yogurt, and honey or agave nectar.

- Blend until smooth and creamy.

- Add ice cubes if desired and blend again until well combined.

Made in the USA
Coppell, TX
23 November 2024